Endorsements

Your Pastor's Wife Needs Your Prayers is an insightful guide into the private life of a pastor's wife, from the prospective of a pastor's wife. This book draws you into understanding the joys and burdens of those women who are called "Pastor's Wives in the 21st Century" and who share the responsibilities of ministry. This is a must read for everyone!

Rev. Dr. Ronald L. Owens,
Senior Pastor of the New Hope Baptist Church of Metuchen, N.J.
Board Member of the National Baptist Convention, U.S.A., Inc.

Your Pastor's Wife Needs Your Prayers is a precise and profound book that addresses the need, support and concern of the pastor's wife in the twenty-first century. Realizing situations or circumstances are sometimes different; this book shows how much that common thread of being the pastor's wife is the same. How do we juggle and balance our lives as a pastor's wife? Simply through faith, love and prayer. These three, but the greatest is PRAYER.

Dr. Beverly Williams Glover
President, International Association of Ministers' Wives
and Ministers' Widows, Inc.

What a wonderful insight into a unique group of women. Informative, inspirational and motivational, *Your Pastor's Wife Needs Your Prayers* is a book long overdue. This book transcends Pastors' Wives. It provides all women with a book of prayers that are so helpful in today's society.

Irene P. Nichols
A Retired High School Principal
Chairman, Million Dollar Capital Campaign

YOUR PASTOR'S *Wife* NEEDS YOUR PRAYERS

A Y A N N A K. M I S H O E - B R O O K E R

WestBow
PRESS®
A DIVISION OF THOMAS NELSON
& ZONDERVAN

Scripture quotations are from the ESV® Bible (The Holy Bible, English Standard Version®), copyright © 2001 by Crossway, a publishing ministry of Good News Publishers. Used by permission. All rights reserved.

WestBow Press books may be ordered through booksellers or by contacting:

WestBow Press
A Division of Thomas Nelson & Zondervan
1663 Liberty Drive
Bloomington, IN 47403
www.westbowpress.com
1 (866) 928-1240

Because of the dynamic nature of the Internet, any web addresses or links contained in this book may have changed since publication and may no longer be valid. The views expressed in this work are solely those of the author and do not necessarily reflect the views of the publisher, and the publisher hereby disclaims any responsibility for them.

Any people depicted in stock imagery provided by Thinkstock are models, and such images are being used for illustrative purposes only. Certain stock imagery © Thinkstock.

ISBN: 978-1-5127-8780-1 (sc)
ISBN: 978-1-5127-8779-5 (e)

Library of Congress Control Number: 2017907956

Print information available on the last page.

WestBow Press rev. date: 05/22/2017

DEDICATION

To my husband, Pastor Johnnie D. Brooker Jr. You are the reason why I was able to write this book. Because of you, I am a pastor's wife!

To the late Erma Jones, the first pastor's wife that made an impact on my life. I never realized how important you were to Saint Mark AME Church in East Orange, New Jersey, until my husband became a pastor. I wish that you were here so that I could tell you all about it!

To the late Leola Johnson. I never got a chance to tell you how much I appreciated you for taking me under your wing when I got married. I had no clue what world I was stepping into. You were definitely a woman of quiet strength and dignity. I miss you.

To Sister Annie Cummings. You gave me the best advice when my husband became a pastor. Wow! I love you.

FOREWORD

It is with great admiration that I am able to participate in a powerful, purposeful, prolific book about prayer. In times of joy and in times of sorrow, prayer is necessary. As a matter of fact, I don't think there is a time when prayer is not needed, because prayer constantly keeps humankind connected to God and God connected to us. Since prayer is our only communication with God and God's with us, I am so grateful that my wife has been inspired to write such a powerful book on prayer. My wife, who is my best friend and the love of my life, and who happens to also be a pastor's wife, has intentionally put together a book on prayer that will help all, and particularly pastors' wives who have journeyed and are journeying through the life of ministry.

We started on this journey in January 2002, when I was licensed to preach at the Greater Mount Moriah Missionary Baptist Church in Newark, New Jersey, and where she became a minister's wife. The journey continued in April 2007, when she became a pastor's wife at the Mount Zion Baptist Church in Dover, New Jersey. Since I have known Ayanna, she has always been a woman of faith and prayer. She prays so fervently for me daily as a pastor, husband, and father that I have been able to experience the results of answered prayers from such a powerful mother and woman of God interceding to God on my behalf. Furthermore, she has been asked to take the lead on many prayer vigils, whether it's at a conference, on a prayer line, or in church, where she has been able to connect with so many people on different levels, seeing the powerful hand of God at work.

Reading *Your Pastor's Wife Needs Your Prayers* will challenge you to be intentional about praying for the pastor's wife and the struggles she goes through on a day-to-day basis. She is a vibrant part of and help to the ministry, her pastor, and her husband. Reading this book will also allow you to see the importance of praying for yourself so you can have the unction and will to pray for others.

I am so excited for you to grasp hold of this wonderful book of prayers because it reminds us that we have joys and sorrows that only prayer can address. Thank you, Ayanna, for allowing the world to peek into your God-given thoughts about prayer and the impact that prayer has on all humankind. I am so proud of you and excited at the same time at what God is doing in your life. I am just happy to be on the journey with you. Thank God for allowing you to put pen on paper in a way that will allow these prayers to last for generations to come.

I love you, honey!

Rev. Johnnie Brooker, BA, MDiv, DMin (c18)

Rev. Johnnie Brooker is the senior pastor of the Mount Zion Baptist Church of Dover, New Jersey, the husband of Ayanna Mishoe-Brooker, and the father of Johnnie Elisha III and Annaya Kai.

ACKNOWLEDGEMENTS

All praise, honor, and glory to my lord and savior, Jesus Christ. I thank him for his grace and mercy in allowing me the opportunity to write this book. Jesus is definitely my rock.

I would like to acknowledge my husband, Pastor Johnnie D. Brooker Jr, and our children, Johnnie Elisha and Annaya Kai. I love you so much. We are truly a team. A family that prays together stays together.

I love you Mommy, Daddy, and big brothers, Luna and Chaka! I am so proud to be a part of the Mishoe family legacy. You mean the world to me.

Thank you Mom and Pop Brooker and the Hodges family. Thank God for joining us together and for raising such a fine Johnnie Delawayne!

To the Leading Lady's Ministry of Mount Zion Baptist Church, former and present members, thank you for supporting me through thick and thin.

Mount Zion Baptist Church, thank you for allowing me the opportunity to be your leading lady.

To all of my prayer partners, prayer warriors, Evangelist Shirley Johnson and Mother Pearl Johnson. Keep on praying without ceasing.

I would also like to acknowledge Dr. Suzan Johnson Cook. She gave me my first writing opportunity without even knowing me personally. I am ever so grateful to her for giving me the indirect push to write this book. Thank you.

I definitely have to acknowledge all of my friends and family who are married to pastors. Thank you for encouraging me. I pray that I have encouraged you along the way too.

I must also acknowledge the members of the Dorcas Alliance of Ministers' Wives and Ministers' Widows, United Ministers' Wives and Ministers' Widows of Newark and Vicinity, and the New Jersey Association of Ministers' Wives and Ministers' Widows, Inc. I look up to you, love you, and thank you for the sisterhood.

PREFACE

On October 12, 2002, I married a minister. He wasn't a minister when we started dating two years prior. In April 2007, he became a pastor, and I became a pastor's wife. At that moment, our lives changed forever because I was now married to him and the church. It's been an interesting journey.

Throughout this course I have become friends with many other pastors' wives. Many of our situations are similar, with slight variations. On the other hand, many of our situations are quite different. Despite the similarities and differences, there is one common thread that is desperately needed in all of our lives: prayer.

Your Pastor's Wife Needs Your Prayers is written in a clear and concise format. Each page begins with a particular reason why the pastor's wife needs your prayers and ends with a prayer that focuses on the reason discussed. You will be surprised at some of the reasons that focus on inner struggles, myths, church hurt, marriage, desires, and so much more.

Even though your pastor's wife may not require a particular prayer focus, other pastors' wives may need it. This is your opportunity to pray for them, too. Prayerfully, this book and your prayers that resonate from it will reach pastors' wives all over the globe. I truly believe that this book can change lives, save lives, save marriages, and dispel untruths that center around pastors' wives.

INTRODUCTION

For the first eighteen years of my life, I grew up in an awesome, family-oriented African Methodist Episcopal church. I admired the pastor, and I adored his wife. She was heavily involved in church activities and very encouraging, and she always looked nice. To be honest, I do not remember her attire, and I do not remember her wearing fancy hats. But I do remember her humbleness. Perhaps my recollection of her is limited because I never considered her as the "pastor's wife." Rather, I always simply considered and referred to her as Sister Jones. Her status never affected my relationship with her.

It wasn't until I started attending a Missionary Baptist church in my late twenties that I began to actually hear the words *pastor's wife.* The term baffled me! Thankfully, I found the pastor's wife of that church to be humble and a woman of quiet strength. She loved her husband and stuck by him. She loved to worship the Lord. These qualities in her stood out to me. While other people called her "Lady Johnson," "first lady," or "the pastor's wife," I simply referred to her as "Sister Johnson" and eventually, "Mother Johnson." Like Sister Jones, Sister Johnson's status never had an impact on our relationship. I always admired her inner beauty. She always had my love and respect.

When my husband was called to pastor, among the very first set of questions that I was asked at the welcome brunch was, "What would you like to be called?" My response was, "Sister Brooker will be just fine." I didn't realize that my response was based on my relationship with Sister Jones and Sister Johnson. I didn't consider myself to be different from anyone else. Without any thought or hesitation, my plan (without any planning) was just to simply be me.

No sooner than my first Sunday worshipping at the church where my husband was called to pastor, I was no longer me. Although my fellow congregants called me "Sister Brooker," as requested, I became known as the pastor's wife. Absent any warning, my name was changed without authorization. My responsibilities changed without preparation. My schedule changed without any say in the matter. My life changed. Fortunately, other pastors' wives in my circle share the same sentiments!

As I reflect back on my time with Sister Jones and Sister Johnson, I wonder what was going on in their lives. What made them humble, quiet, faithful, and encouraging? They carried the same qualities every Sunday that I saw them in church. Were they always like that? Were they only like that on Sunday mornings? Did their lives change forever like my life did once my husband became a pastor? What were their struggles, joys, highs, and lows? How did they handle problems, people in the church, their children, their husbands, and conflicts? I wish they were still living so that I could speak with them about my concerns. Was anyone praying for them? I certainly wasn't. To be honest, I never thought about praying for any pastor's wife until I became one.

Your Pastor's Wife Needs Your Prayers invites you to experience what goes on in the heart, mind, life, and marriage of a pastor's wife. Most importantly, this book encourages you to pray for your pastor's wife. Although your pastor's wife may not need every prayer included in this book, pray for another pastor's wife who may be in need of the prayer. The effective, fervent prayer of a righteous man avails much (James 5:16).

CONTENTS

to be
point of vie

Pray [prei]

to ask ear

God, for a

Prayer 1

THE PASTOR HAS TO CHOOSE BETWEEN HIS WIFE AND THE CHURCH

Oftentimes, plans are made, and then suddenly interrupted. The pastor gets a call—while he and his wife are enjoying their long-awaited alone time together—and the caller advises him that a member of the church is in critical condition and needs him to come to the hospital right away. The pastor is asked to officiate at a funeral that happens to be on the same day as his wife's class reunion. A couple asked the pastor to marry them on the same date the pastor's family planned a vacation, which has been in the works for almost a year. The Christmas pageant is on the day of his wife's fiftieth birthday. Conflicts! The pastor has to choose—the church or his wife?

🙏 Let's Pray

Dear Lord, I didn't realize the effect of the church's needs on the pastor's wife or her family. Help me to be more considerate and understanding. Help the church to be considerate and understanding. Please be with the pastor's wife as she endures whichever decision her husband makes. May his decision be led by God, and may she receive it in Jesus's name. I also ask that you restore and multiply whatever time or bonding has been lost or broken as a result of the decision. I also ask that any backlash from the decision cease. Amen.

Prayer 2

THE MARRIAGE IS UNDER ATTACK

The marriage between a pastor and his wife is no different from any other marriage that has been ordained by God. There are no special perks from heaven for being married to a pastor. The pastor and his wife have ups and downs too. Yet the pastor and his wife have to continue to be "on point" in order to lead people effectively.

🙏 Let's Pray

Dear Lord, I understand that a pastor cannot lead a church if his own house is not in order. Be with my pastor and his wife right now. Fix whatever has been broken. Sew together whatever has become unstitched. Bring them back to what brought them together in the first place. Allow them to focus on you and to keep you at the center of the marriage. Cover the marriage. Let no weapons that are formed against them prosper. Be with them. Keep her covered, strong, and faithful unto you. Amen.

Prayer 3
ENCOURAGEMENT NEEDED

*Y*es! The pastor's wife needs to be encouraged too. She needs motivation. She needs prayer. She needs to hear words of encouragement: "I wish you the best!", "You can do it!", "Don't get discouraged!", "Hold on," "I appreciate you," "Thank you," and "Is there anything I can do for you?" Yes. The pastor's wife needs encouragement too.

🙏 Let's Pray

Dear Lord, thank you for the pastor's wife, and thank you for all that she does. She gives of her time and makes so many sacrifices in order to be a help to God's people. Lift her up as she gets weary along the journey. Continue to keep her eyes steadied on you, which is where her help comes from. Remind her that only what she does for Christ will last. Bless her for being a blessing. Lift her head up when she feels down. Give her a push if she feels stagnant. Change the hearts of those who couldn't care less. May I be more attentive to her needs. Amen.

Prayer 4

THE PASTOR IS CHEATING ON HER

Hmm! Pastors are highly sought after by other women. Why? Perhaps it's the suit and tie, or maybe it's the position and title. Although there is nothing "cute" about being a pastor, there are women who are on the outside but desire to be on the inside. Unfortunately, some pastors don't always know how to handle these predators and end up falling short. Note, however, that it takes two to tango.

☙ Let's Pray

Dear Lord, I'm praying for my pastor's wife right now. If she has fallen victim to the nonsense of her husband and another woman, I pray that you reveal to her what needs to be revealed and that she act accordingly. Lord, you don't desire divorce, but your Word says adultery is grounds for it.[1] If this is the route she is led to take, please be with her in the process. However, Lord, my desire is that healing and forgiveness take place right now. Don't allow other people, such as the church members, to cloud her decisions. May she think and act wisely. Lord, allow love to abound right now. Hug her tight right now. For you said in your Word that you would never leave or forsake her.[2] Amen.

Prayer 5
SHE JUST WANTS TO BE HERSELF

*P*astor's wives are sometimes deemed as superwomen who are *supposed* to do what they do. Not so! Let's start with the fact that her responsibility is to her husband, like in any other godly marriage. She should never be expected to do anything, say anything, be a part of any ministry, or go anywhere just because she is the pastor's wife. Let her be herself. She has a name other than "the pastor's wife."

🙏 Let's Pray

Dear Lord, forgive me for having so many expectations of what a pastor's wife should or should not be doing. Forgive me for being in her business and even trying to indirectly dictate her life. At the same time, permit her to find her space and be comfortable in it. Prevent her from falling into diverse temptations and succumbing to the pressures and expectations of church members and traditions. I thank you in advance for a church that will be supportive of her decisions, which are godly and in accordance with your will. Amen.

Prayer 6

THE PASTOR IS SICK

*I*t's tough on a wife when her husband is sick. The plot thickens when the husband is sick—and he's the pastor! The wife has to answer to the church, care for the family and for the husband, and in some instances care for the church, if she is acting in the capacity of an associate pastor. Clearly, she has to somehow juggle demands and fulfill expectations.

🙏 Let's Pray

Dear Lord, come to the aid of the pastor's wife right now. In the name of Jesus, order her steps. Strengthen her right now, and remind her that when she is weak, you are strong. Bring her closer to you. Give her wisdom to seek help, as necessary. Take away any pride that is present. Thank you for your keeping power as she handles the responsibilities that come her way. Hold her up. Maintain her stamina as she wards off any germ or disease that is lingering and attempting to latch onto her. Be a fence around her. Amen.

Prayer 7

SHE FEELS IGNORED BY HER HUSBAND

There are times when the pastor's wife needs her husband to be her pastor. Similarly, there are times when the pastor's wife needs her husband to be her husband. Both roles are twenty-four hours a day, seven days a week. He takes care of everyone in the church, but is he taking care of her and her needs?

🙏 Let's Pray

Dear Lord, I thank you for all the attention the pastor has given our church. Now I ask for a shift, so that he can focus on his wife just as much as he focuses on the church. Let her feel him again, and let him fulfill what she has been missing. Reignite the fire. Reignite the passion. Turn his attention to her beauty. Fix his mind to never forget her needs, wants, and desires. Open up portals of communication. Change the conversation from church talk to talk about the two of them as a couple. Thank you for the spark and smile that you are putting on the face of the pastor's wife as I pray this prayer. Amen.

Prayer 8

IT IS HER BIRTHDAY

*B*irthdays are only celebrated once a year. Why not celebrate the birthday of the pastor's wife? Honor and shower her with your love and appreciation. It's allowed. Let her know that she is appreciated. Acknowledge her birthday. After all, when she's happy, the pastor is happy!

🙏 Let's Pray

Dear Lord, thank you for gifting the pastor's wife with another year of life. Thank you for your grace and mercy that you have bestowed upon her. Thank you for this day of celebration. Thank you for how you have kept her. Thank you for keeping every promise that you have made to her. Engage her prayers on this day. Answer her by giving her the desires of her heart. I pray that this year be a year of new beginnings, advancements, rejoicing, and encouragement, and fewer challenges. Thank you for this day to rejoice and celebrate her. Amen.

Prayer 9

ISOLATION

$\mathcal{P}$astor's wives are unique. Unfortunately, with this uniqueness come many myths and misconceptions. As a result, she can become isolated. For example, no one wants to include her on their invitation list because dancing is involved. Another example: certain conversations are removed from her presence in fear that she may tell the pastor. Last example: she is denied certain gifts she may really appreciate because people feel as though she doesn't need the item or wouldn't wear it or use it. Isolation hurts. Please note that pastors' wives do more than just go to church on Sunday.

🙏 Let's Pray

Dear Lord, forgive me for putting my pastor's wife in a box or on a pedestal. Help me to look beyond the surface and outside of the box. Help me to realize that she is human and that isolation hurts, whether intentional or unintentional. Give me the wisdom and discernment to know the difference. Forgive me for situations where I could have made her feel welcomed and involved but chose not to. Work with me so that I can be myself around her. Encourage me to communicate with her on different levels and not just in times of need or distress. Amen.

Prayer 10

SHE IS SICK

*H*mmm. Yes. The pastor's wife does get sick from time to time. Perhaps the diagnosis is simple. Perhaps the diagnosis is critical. Either way, prayers are needed for healing, strength, encouragement, and protection around the family and the marriage. Sometimes congregants don't care at all. Sometimes pastors' wives endure the sickness alone and forbid anyone to know the extent of the illness (even the pastor). Prayers are especially needed when other women use this opportunity to "make moves" on the pastor.

🙏 Let's Pray

Dear Lord, I ask that you heal any ailment that has been attacking the body of my pastor's wife. I ask that you get down to the nitty-gritty of it right now so that she can get back on her feet and continue to do great work in your kingdom. Restore her body, soul, and mind. Be with her mentally, physically, and spiritually. Encourage her family through this time. Give them strength and the know-how to tend to her needs. Keep the enemy at a distance as healing takes place. Let no weapon formed against her marriage prosper. Amen.

Prayer 11

SHE IS GOING THROUGH A SITUATION

The pastor's wife is human. She goes through situations. She has issues too. Some pastors' wives express these situations through their countenance or actions. Others hide it under the "hat" to a point where no one can recognize that a problem exists. The latter is usually the typical expression of a pastor's wife. Maybe it's a good thing, or perhaps it can be to her detriment. Perhaps she doesn't want to disclose anything for fear that she will be talked about, scrutinized, questioned, or scorned. After all, the pastor's wife is usually misconceived or wrongly labeled as "Ms. Perfect."

🙏 Let's Pray

Dear Lord, I'm not able to discern whether or not my pastor's wife is going through a situation right now. If she is going through something, I trust that you are there in the midst of the situation. I trust that you are walking beside her. I pray she looks to you, which is where her help comes from. I pray you stick to her closer than any brother or sister. Insist that she make the right decision and seek the right help, as necessary. Keep her as only you know how. Amen.

Prayer 12

SHE WANTS TO WALK AWAY FROM THE CHURCH

*C*hurch can become overwhelming. Church can become unbearable at times. Things happen in the church, which can cause "church hurt." The pastor's wife experiences church hurt too. She is always expected to hang in there or turn the other cheek or be the first to forgive. There comes a time when enough is enough. Can she really walk away from the church? It's not that simple, but unfortunately, it happens.

🙏 Let's Pray

Dear Lord, I pray right now that you plant the feet of my pastor's wife on solid ground. I pray that you keep her committed to the work of Jesus Christ. Lord, whatever it is that is causing her to raise her hands up and want to throw in the towel, I ask that you change the motion of those hands into a "hallelujah" of praise. Be a fence around her. Prevent her from doing anything foolish. I realize that weapons have been formed, but I believe that they shall not prosper because your Word says so.[3] I believe that this battle will be victorious and will end in her favor. Amen.

Prayer 13

SHE HAS AN ISSUE WITH ANOTHER CHURCH MEMBER

*S*ome church members are stuck in their own ways. Some are stuck on tradition, and some are stuck on position. Some are strategically planted by Satan to cause trouble and lead an attack on the pastor's wife. Some plots are more subtle than others. How does the pastor's wife deal with this? She is not expected to lash out. Rather, she is expected to carry herself in a dignified, ladylike, Christian manner at all times. Is this fair? It can actually be hurtful at times.

🙏 Let's Pray

Dear Lord, thank you for coming down to this earth and walking with us in the flesh. Since you walked with us in the flesh, you experienced everything that we go through: hurt, pain, envy, strife, criticism, sensitivity, lies—you name it! Lord, I don't want my pastor's wife to endure these battles. Therefore, I pray that you turn the situation around for your glory. Shed light on this dark situation. Remove the dark cloud that is overpowering her. Comfort her, keep her mind, guard her heart, and bridle her tongue. You said that our enemies will be a footstool.[4] As a result, I thank you for the elevation you are granting in her life. Allow her to fear no evil because you are with her. You are her rock, her buckler, her shield. Thank you for fixing "it." Amen.

Prayer 14

SHE HAS A CALLING OVER HER LIFE THAT IS BEING OVERLOOKED

*I*t is quite possible that a pastor's wife has a special calling over her life too. What happens when she has a calling to preach, a calling to teach, a calling to usher, a calling to lead a ministry? Is her calling stifled? Is her calling supported by her husband? Is her calling being put on hold? There are pastors who believe that their wives should just sit on the front pew every Sunday, look stunning, and sit silently. If her calling is overlooked, major conflicts, both internal and external, can erupt.

🙏 Let's Pray

Dear Lord, thank you for the calling on the life of the pastor's wife, for it is your will. Let thy will be done. I pray that you soften the stony hearts and minds of those who are not in agreement with her calling and are disobedient to your will. May she successfully acomplish all that she has been destined to do. May she do what you have formed her to do since she was in her mother's womb. May she proceed with what you have equipped her to do. Your grace will never lead us to a place where you cannot keep us. Cover her. Provide her with the support that she needs. May she be respected wherever her feet tread. May she do it all for your glory and honor. Amen.

Prayer 15

FEELING OVERWHELMED

The pastor's wife has to wear many hats. She has a career. She's a mother. She's a wife. She's a sister. She's a daughter. She's an aunt. She's often the women's ministry leader. People look to her for spiritual guidance. She is the pastor's helpmeet. Whew! All of this can be overwhelming at times. Life can definitely be demanding.

🙏 Let's Pray

Dear Lord, please permit the pastor's wife to receive balance in her life. Order her steps. Lead the way for her. Direct her path. Clear her mind, remind her that prayer is the answer, and let her feel the love and compassion you have for her. Also, encourage her to cast all her burdens on you. Open up the line of trust so that she can put it all in your hands. Remove all worry and fear from her. We cast it all out and bind it up in the name of Jesus. Amen.

Prayer 16

EXPECTATIONS OF THE CHURCH

*U*nattainable expectations of the pastor's wife run rampant in the church. What's even more astonishing is that people who do not attend church regularly have expectations of the pastor's wife too! The pastor's wife is expected to wear a hat, dress up all of the time, be nice at all times, deliver all messages to the pastor, and look pretty. Really? Please take note that there are no "pastor's wives must do …" guidelines.

🙏 Let's Pray

Dear Lord, please forgive me if my expectancy levels have been at a peak. Please forgive others who have taken her to that place too. Let us remember that she is only to be who you have destined her to be. Thank you for her destiny, which you have already ordained and sought to be so. She is your child, your servant, your vessel, and your creation. I humbly ask that you give me a better understanding of the Scripture, "Present your bodies a living sacrifice unto Him, for this is your reasonable service."[5] Amen.

Prayer 17

PROTECTIVE MOTHER

The children are a mother's top priority. The love, concern, and intensity of the relationship is no different for the children of the pastor's wife. Like a bear, she is protective of her cubs. You want to hear a lion roar? Mess with her cubs! Children are children and are expected to do what children do. The expectancy level of a preacher's kid (PK) shouldn't be any different. Be mindful of what you say about a PK, especially if it's negative. It's only natural for the pastor's wife to respond. As a mother, wouldn't you?

🙏 Let's Pray

Dear Lord, thank you for gifting the pastor's wife with children. Thank you for them. Protect them and keep them from all hurt, harm, and danger. I express my gratitude to you for allowing them the freedom to be children and to grow in the knowledge, wisdom, and stature of Jesus Christ. Spare them from unnecessary attacks and opinions, and from unreasonable expectations. Give people the understanding to treat the children of the pastor the same way they would treat their own children who are growing up in the Word. Lord, I also ask that you minister to the pastor's wife as she ministers to the welfare and wellbeing of her children. Amen.

Prayer 18

SHE DOESN'T FEEL LIKE DRESSING THE PART

In the traditional churches, pastors' wives usually wear fancy dresses or dress suits, big hats, high heels, and pantyhose on Sunday morning. Should they be expected to dress up and look good wherever they go? Pastor's wives should at least be allowed to go to the grocery store in jeans, sneakers, and no makeup! Is there a written dress code anywhere stating how pastor's wives must dress? Absolutely not! Try not to scrutinize her when she doesn't feel like dressing the part of the unwritten dress code.

🙏 Let's Pray

Dear Lord, thank you for the inner beauty of the pastor's wife. Pardon me for only paying attention to the outer appearance and not focusing on her inner beauty and qualities. Forgive me for talking about her when she doesn't look the way I think she should look. Lord, let her be comfortable with whatever she wears, and may she not get caught up and consumed with worldly thoughts. May she not feel bound and end up in debt due to trying to meet the standards of others. Thank you for the style that she possesses, and may it always be pleasing in your sight. Amen.

Prayer 19

VICTIM OF GOSSIP

People are always going to have something to say about the pastor's wife. Regardless of how nice she is, regardless of how quiet she is, regardless of how beautiful she looks, people are always going to have something to say about her. Gossip hurts. Negative comments hurt. Don't be a part of the conversations as such. Instead, walk away.

🙏 Let's Pray

Dear Lord, please forgive me for talking about the pastor's wife. Please forgive others who talk negatively about her too. Change my mindset. Bridle my tongue, and let my words edify. Let the words I speak be acceptable to your ear and a sweet aroma to your nostrils. If she has been hurt by anything that has been said about her or to her, heal her wounded spirit. Let forgiveness prevail. Let love truly reside within. Amen.

Prayer 20

SHE HAS A VISION THAT HAS SUCCESSFULLY LAUNCHED

All attention is usually on the pastor's vision for the congregation. It should be, because he is the pastor of that church. However, there are actually dreams that are conceived in some pastors' wives that expand beyond the walls of the church. Yes. The pastor's wife can be pregnant with possibilities too. Do you abort them, or do you allow them to be born and mature?

🙏 Let's Pray

Dear Lord, thank you for the vision that you have birthed in the pastor's wife. I pray that it takes flight and travels to every destination you have intended for it to go. Don't allow her vision to be delayed. Don't allow her vision to crash. May other people get onboard and be in agreement. Don't allow anyone to hijack her joy or interfere with the plans you have for her life. Thank you for her life. May we all enjoy the ride. Amen.

Prayer 21

OUT ON ASSIGNMENT

Thank God for pastors who believe in female ministers. Thank God for pastors who do not mind if their wives are invited to speak or preach at other churches or church-related programs. Thank God for the gift that she possesses and the ability to do what she does. There are definitely times when both are on assignment at the same time. Thank God for those who are able to support her when the pastor cannot due to church calendar conflicts. Thank God even for the times she has to go on assignment alone.

🙏 Let's Pray

Dear Lord, thank you for the gift you have given to the pastor's wife. I appreciate the fact that she uses it to your glory. Thank you for accompanying her not only on assignment, but also in the preparation. Be a fence around her wherever her feet tread. If she has to travel alone, give her protection and strength. As long as she is giving you the glory, I know that you are attentive to her needs and definitely in support of what she has been called to do. Smile upon her. Shine upon her. If there is anything that I can do to encourage her, compel me to do so without hesitation. Amen.

Prayer 22

SHE HAS STOPPED COMING TO CHURCH

*U*h-oh! What happened? Why did she stop coming to church? Did she have a disagreement with her husband? Did she have a disagreement with someone at the church? Is she upset with God? Is she attending another church now? Either way, something has been broken that needs fixing.

🙏 Let's Pray

Dear Lord, my pastor's wife has stopped coming to church. Instead of me focusing on why, I am praying that her worship has not been hindered and ask that you correct whatever has gone wrong and fix whatever has been broken. Heal wounded hearts. Clear the minds of foolishness. Let forgiveness prevail. Let peace and love abound. Set the atmosphere for new beginnings. Hold her head up high so that she may feel your grace and mercy. Bring her back "home." Amen.

Prayer 23

THE PASTOR PUTS EVERYONE BEFORE HER

The pastor has a lot of responsibility. He has to tend to his family, the needs of the congregation, and the issues of the community. The calendar fills up rather quickly, and there never seems to be enough time in a twenty-four-hour day. There are congregants who desire more attention than others, and many times, congregants expect the pastor to be readily available in a microwave moment. Situations such as this can cause a strain on the pastor's marriage, especially when the pastor puts everyone before her (the pastor's wife).

🙏 Let's Pray

Dear Lord, I come on behalf of the pastor's wife right with a pressing concern. She has been neglected. As a result of the neglect, she has been emotionally wounded. Heal her and restore her. In addition, I ask that you open the mind of her husband so that he will realize the impact and strain that his schedule has on her. Show him how to prioritize, sympathize, and empathize. Bring the home to his remembrance at all times, and instill in him the invaluable meaning of "He who finds himself a wife finds himself a good thing."[6] Amen.

Prayer 24

SHE DESIRES TO DO MORE

*I*t's a blessing to have a talented pastor's wife. It's even more of a blessing when she wants to give birth to a seed of dreams and desires that have been planted in her heart. The Word says that we ought not to sit on our gifts.[7] What happens when the seed isn't allowed to blossom? What happens when she is not given the proper resources to nurture the seed? Does the sun even shine in her direction?

🙏 Let's Pray

Dear Lord, thank you for the vision that has been planted in my pastor's wife. I thank you in advance for sanctioning it to come to pass. Thank you for permitting her goals to be fruitful and fruit-bearing. I pray that whatever she does be done with a spirit of excellence and to glorify your name. Forbid her to sit on her gift. I pray that others bubble over with excitement and lend a helping a helping hand if necessary. Bind up any unnecessary chatter. Be a fence around her, and let no weapon formed against her prosper. Amen.

Prayer 25

JUGGLING HER CAREER WITH CHURCH OBLIGATIONS

There was a time when the pastor's wife did not work a secular job. Times have drastically changed. More often than not, you will find that the pastor's wife is not only working, but has a stable career. Some careers are more demanding than others, which may cause her to miss or be tardy for events that are on the church calendar. Some careers may even require her to miss Sunday morning worship services. This isn't the most comfortable position.

🙏 Let's Pray

Dear Lord, thank you for providing the pastor's wife with a thriving career. Thank you for equipping and empowering her to do what she has worked toward. Fix her schedule so that she does not have to do the juggling. I pray that she consult you first before she makes any work-related decision. Remove the stress, anxieties, guilt, fear, and worries that she may have about what others may think. Order her steps. Fill her home with understanding. May they all be of one accord and considerate of each other's needs. Most importantly, may she always put you first. Amen.

Prayer 26

WHEN HER MINISTRY IS FLOURISHING

*I*t's a blessing when God has gifted the pastor's wife to lead a ministry. It's a blessing when she has been given wings and is spreading them wide. As a Christian grows higher in Christ, he or she faces more challenges. Some of the challenges the pastor's wife faces when the ministry is flowing are opposition, lack of support, conflicts, jealousy, and unnecessary chatter. This shouldn't be so. Let it flow!

🙏 Let's Pray

Dear Lord, thank you for the ministry that the pastor's wife leads. Thank you for the opportunity that you have given her to do what she does. Thank you for her motivation, despite the odds that may come against her. I pray that this ministry you have allowed her to lead continue to flourish. I declare that your name will be edified and you be glorified in all things and at all times. Provide her with the support she needs. Equip her. Renew her strength daily. Hamper her from getting weary on the journey, and thwart anything that tries to detour her from her destiny. Amen.

Prayer 27

CONTEMPLATING DIVORCE

*A*ny marriage has its ups and downs. Unfortunately, there are too many downs in some marriages, and in some cases, they far outweigh the ups. When this happens, wanting out of the marriage becomes a top-of-the-list option. Contemplating a separation or divorce can put the pastor's wife in a difficult dilemma because in addition to having to face her family and friends, she has to battle the reaction of the church. Does she stay in the marriage to keep an appearance, or does she continue with the so-called ugly, taboo church word, *divorce?*

🙏 Let's Pray

Dear Lord, I'm praying for the pastor's wife who is struggling with whether or not she should divorce the pastor. I realize the church congregants can be affected by breakup. However, I ask that you steer her clear of clouded decisions. I pray that she be released from the thought of what the church may think. Clear her mind so that she may think clearly, rationally, and in line with your will. Amen.

Prayer 28

"CHURCHED OUT"

The pastor's wife is expected to be at every worship service. She is expected to support every program. She is expected to support everybody. She is expected to be involved. Her demanded presence can lead to exhaustion and sometimes, resentment. Yes. The pastor's wife gets "churched out" sometimes.

🙏 Let's Pray

Dear Lord, I am grateful for freedom and freedom of choice. I forget sometimes that the pastor's wife may not have the flexibility of choice. Grant her wisdom, and let her work according to the assignment you have given her to abide by. Energize, strengthen, and lead her. Reveal to her what she should and should not be doing. Bring about an understanding to those who don't realize the strain and struggle. Keep her committed to you, and prevent her from getting caught up and "churched out." Amen.

Prayer 29

RESENTED ONLY BECAUSE SHE WAS NOT THE FIRST "FIRST LADY"

The title *first lady* is a title that many have strayed away from. It's difficult to call the pastor's wife "first lady" if she is not the first wife. It can also be difficult to call the pastor's wife "first lady" if the church was very fond of the pastor's first or prior wife. Regardless of how the current pastor's wife came to be, we must still respect her as the pastor's wife. Let go of the resentment!

🙏 Let's Pray

Dear Lord, forgive me for the resentment that I have toward the pastor's wife. Forgive me for giving her a hard time just because she is not the wife that I knew and formed a bond with. Give me a fresh start so that I can see in her what you see in her. I refuse to judge. I bind up all plots and schemes that have been formed against her. I plan to be a help to her and not a hindrance to her. I pray for peace, love, harmony, and unity. Lord, it's all in your hands, and I know that you know best. Amen.

ENDNOTES

1   Matthew 19:9 (ESV): "And I say to you: whoever divorces his wife, except for sexual immorality, and marries another, commits adultery."

2   Hebrews 13:5 (ESV): "Keep your life free from love of money, and be content with what you have, for he has said, "I will never leave you or forsake you."

3   Isaiah 54:17 (ESV): "No weapon that is fashioned against you shall succeed, and you shall confute every tongue that rises against you in judgment. This is the heritage of the servants of the Lord and their vindication from me, declares the Lord."

4   Acts 2:34–35 (ESV): "For David did not ascend into the heavens, but he himself says, 'The Lord said to my Lord, "Sit at my right hand, until I make your enemies your footstool."'"

5   Romans 12:1(ESV): "I appeal to you therefore, brothers, by the mercies of God, to present your bodies as a living sacrifice, holy and acceptable to God, which is your spiritual worship."

6   Proverbs 18:22 (ESV): "He who finds a wife finds a good thing and obtains favor from the Lord."

7   Romans 12:6 (ESV): "Having gifts that differ according to the grace given to us, let us use them: if prophecy, in proportion to our faith."

ABOUT THE AUTHOR

Minister Ayanna Kai Mishoe-Brooker Esq. is the proud daughter of Mr. and Mrs. Luna I. Mishoe. She is happily married to Reverend Johnnie D. Brooker Jr, pastor of Mount Zion Baptist Church in Dover, New Jersey. Together, they have one amazing son, Johnnie Elisha III, and one vivacious daughter, Annaya Kai.

The importance of a good education was instilled in Minister Brooker at a very early age. She truly believes in education and encourages all youth to do their best in school. She is proud to be a product of the East Orange school system, beginning at what was then Elmwood Elementary and graduating from Clifford J. Scott High School as valedictorian. Upon graduating from high school, Minister Brooker was accepted at Embry-Riddle Aeronautical University, where she received her degree in aviation business administration. Aspiring to become an attorney, she received a juris doctorate degree from Seton Hall University in 2001. Also, very early in life, Minister Brooker knew that she had been called to evangelism. She did receive a master of divinity degree with an emphasis in pastoral counseling from Andersonville Theological Seminary in May 2014.

In 2003, she and a partner opened a law office in East Orange, New Jersey. She put her practice on hold to accept a position at AIG in New York handling employment practices and liability claims. She saved the company millions of dollars in settlements. After seven years of service with AIG, she is now with Chubb in New Jersey.

She truly understands the importance of giving back to her community. She is a graduate and lifelong member of Eagle Flight Squadron, Inc., a not-for-profit aviation school for urban youth based in East Orange, New Jersey. She continues to work with the program as a major supporter, volunteer, and contributor. She is a member of the Saint Barnabas Medical Center Neonatal Intensive Care Unit (NICU) parent advisory board and volunteers in the NICU on a regular basis. She is also vice president of the Home School Association executive board at Aquinas Academy, Livingston, New Jersey.

Minister Brooker truly believes in God and is deeply rooted in her faith. She has a keen focus on missionary work and ministering to others. She has preached at numerous retreats and revivals and has taught at several workshops and conferences. She enjoys encouraging people of all ages to reach their full potential and to utilize the Holy Spirit that God has endowed them with. She also enjoys and is committed to praying for others, visiting the sick and shut in, and providing for those in need.

She is truly a woman of many talents and gifts and does not mind sharing her thoughts, experiences, and words of wisdom. More importantly, she not only desires that you reach for your goals, but also that you achieve them. She would like to leave you with these words: **"Don't be afraid to take the leap. Step out on faith. Do it. Challenge yourself. Turn your setbacks into your comebacks. You can do it!"**

Printed in the United States
By Bookmasters